Demons

BY EMILY WATERS

Contents

He Whistles a Happy Tune

He smiles as he shoots,

Frowns as he looks,

He looks away and pretends to forget,

Watching civilians stare ahead,
They are horrified.   So is he,

Yet he pretends,

Whistles a happy tune,

Talks to his friend,

Who is soon to be gone,

It's lonely, it's scary; he can handle it.

He whistles a happy tune,

Shoots another man,

Who is he fighting for now?

How can conflict be solved with bullets and wars?

The people stare on in terror,

One man shoots another,

It all has to end in horror,

He looks around,

Bodies surrounding him,

He whistles a happy tune,

And pretends once again,

As he whistles a happy tune.

Maze

The demons whisper into my mind,

And I do not know how to fight.

Kicking and screaming,

I tear apart my flesh,

Hoping to rid the pain in which their words cause,   But
to no avail.
Instead,

I become more and more lost,   As

my demons grow,

Stronger than I ever imagined,

They whisper doubts into my mind,
And knock me down whenever I try to rise,

How can it be, that my demons are stronger than I am?

That my own mind,

Has pushed me into the depths of its maze?

I am trapped in a dead end,

And there is no way out,

Except maybe for that rope hanging from the wall,

A tiny bit of hope continues to survive,

As I fight with my last bit of strength,

Fighting until

I finally cannot.

Fitting in

She puts on a fake smile,

As she tries to hide,

The darkness in which claws its way around her heart,

She puts on some make up,

And tries to look pretty,

Attempting once again,

To fit in,

People are whispering insults behind her,

A few brave enough to whisper into her ears,

She tries her best to fit in,

She cannot run and hide,

Cannot let her fear consume her,

But yet their words haunt her,

As the demons inside of her head,

Whisper words to her heart,

She wipes away her tears,

Yet they continue to fall; the scars have been made,

And now,

She cannot undo the pain,

Or even the temptation of it,

Fear of falling further consumes her,

And any chances of fitting in are in shreds surrounding her.

Whispers and Stares

Whispers and stares,

Are all that she knows,

Watching her they laugh,

And so, she falls apart,
How could they ever love her?

How could they ever see?

They do so much harm,

As they whisper and stare,

Watching as she breaks,

Not knowing the pain,

Not understanding the desperation,

Not understanding the illness,

She's just being dramatic after all,

One thing and she breaks,

A tear escapes her eye,

So petty and so childish,

Yet she can't help but care,

Why don't they like her? What
can she do?
Try to be someone else,

But what good does that ever do?

So behind closed doors she cries,

And all they see is the façade,

She's fine, doing much better,

But really inside,

She's drowning more than ever.

Why I Try

You ask me why I try,

And I do not really know,

For every time that I try,

It leaves me more broken every time,

Sometimes I think that I have had enough,

Yet I still have to get up,

And try to believe that it is all going to be good,

Yet I don't really know why,

I care for people around me,

I love and trust with everything that I am,

Even though every time that I try,

I am disappointed and let down,

I still get up every day,

And pretend to be okay,

I don't know why I do,

But maybe someday I will.

Darkness

Sitting in the dark,

All that she can do is cry,

Trapped, alone and desperate,

Throat too dry to scream,

Mascara lines down her cheeks,

She is broken beyond repair,

Yet still she cannot move,

Locked away in the dark she has to stay,

So terrified, so cold,

The darkness is suffocating as it keeps her chained up,

She cannot seem to move,

She cannot stand up to escape,

All that she can do is cry,

A prisoner to her own mind,

Lazy to the eyes of others,

Messy and unorganised,

Whilst the real her is lost somewhere deep inside,

Tears continue to fall,

As she loses herself more each day

Desperate Eyes

Their eyes,

So desperate and broken,

The light has gone, disappeared,

They are depressed,

They used to be so happy.

So full of light

But now they are depressed,

Confused and Conflicted,
Sad, lost, helpless,
How am I the only one that see's through their smiles?

Their screams,

So loud,

They want our help,

Just someone to talk to,

They are screaming for help; how can you not hear?

Their hearts,

So broken,

They don't think that they will ever heal,

Everything seems lost to them,   Tell

me why can you not see?!

Their eyes are clearly desperate,

Their screams so loud,

And their hearts don't seem to ever heal,   How

am I the only one that notices?

To Be Nowhere

I just want to cry,

To hide and be nowhere,

I cannot explain why,

For it makes no sense at all,

And I don't think that anyone would understand,

Or try to pretend to care,

I just want to be alone,

Yet when I am I don't,

When I am around people,

I feel like I'm too fake,

Yet when no one is there,

It feels too real,

And all I want to do,

Is to cry and be invisible,

And to be somewhere,

So far away,

Or maybe just to be absolutely nowhere at all.

Rise up Again

Rise up through the darkness,

Push the thoughts away,

You are worthy of this life,

You are worthy of love,

All seems lost right now,

A cloud of darkness hovering,

Walking through hell isn't easy,

But these are the moments that make a person,

You can't change the past,

No matter how much easier it would make the present,

But you can rise up again,

You can get back up,

The darkness does not define you,

But how you rise up again after it destroys you.

Empty

Their faces empty,

Hearts broken,

The light is lost,

And they are surrounded by grey,

They don't care anymore,

Their will to be someone gone,

Their will to be alive disappearing,

There is something missing,

They have no hope,

They don't believe they are loved,

Stuck in a trance,

They can't move,

They stare at the ceiling,

Wondering how and when they lost their way,

They can't bring themselves to eat,

They have no tears left,

Their throats are too dry to scream,

They can't sleep,

Can't function,

And as they slowly wither away,

They are shunned by society,

Being told they are lazy,

When really, they are just empty,

Hopelessness consuming them after enduring so much pain,

They have lost themselves

Gone

So many emotions,

All of them bad,

Unwanted and unheard,

There is a deafening silence,

And nothing will ever be the same again, emptiness and numbness,

The beginning is the worst.

I look for you on the street,

Expect to see your text on my phone,

Before the horrific reality sets in,

Gone, dead and at peace; you have left me,

The disease took you away,

I think the worst is over, I have accepted it,

But then I see your casket,

I hear words and stories,

I hear music and I cry,

Breaking as I know,

That I may never see you again,

My best friend,

My hero,

Gone, forever lost to me,

Still with me in my heart and bittersweet memories, yet you are not in this world anymore,

The only salvation, the only peace and clarity that I have,

Is the hope that you are no longer suffering,

My Demons

The demons are surrounding me,

There are so many of them,

They force me to remember my sins,

They make me think about how cruel this world is,

And remind me how much most people do not care,

They yell words at me and laugh at my expense,

Laughing through my panic attacks and through the pain,

Whilst they constantly push me deeper into the dark,

Into a world of depression where thoughts of suicide invade my mind, They laugh as I come closer to pulling the trigger.
They whisper into my ears that soon they will win this fight,

That really,

In a way they already have,

They chuckle as I pretend to be okay,

Their sinister smiles haunt me as I try to push them away from me,

I tell myself again and again,

I cannot let them win,

Yet deep down I know that they already have.

Add Fuel to the Fire

The world is red,

The sky is dark,

All that I can hear are screams,

Cries,

People begging for mercy, Begging
for help.
But the people are heartless,

As they shoot their opponents,

Fight fire with fire,   Fight
with one another, To the
death.
The world has become so dark,   Or

has it always been this way?

I'm surrounded by the colour red,

The future looks dark and empty,

I'm scared to go ahead.

All I hear is screams

STOP.

You are just adding fuel to the fire,

Shoot them if you have to,

But remember that you are no better than them.

Tear Each Other Down

Screams are heard from around them,

As they carry on the fight,

Another body falls,

Can anyone be saved?

Darkness continues to strive,

Destroying each soul in its wake,

Everyone is damaged,
How can we survive like this?

We cannot seem to be able to defeat the darkness,

To defeat the empty feeling that consumes each and every one of us,

And so, we just fight one another,

Maybe that could create the light,

Bullets and punches are heard,

As the screams grow louder,

In the depths of the darkness,

No one can see a way out,

And so, we scream at one another,

Tearing each other down,

As each and every one of us tries to find an exit,

From the never ending dark.

Black and White

The world is dark,

And I cannot see where I am,

All I can see or hear,

Are the demons who are whispering in my ear.

Soon I start to see,

Though only in black and white,

They all have perfect lives,

How could they possibly understand the heartache that I feel?

The need to fit in

The desperation that consumes me?

Soon,

The grey starts to appear,

And finally, I start to realise that they are not so perfect after all,

I am not the only one,

Who the demons are whispering to,

It doesn't really matter however,

Because after all they are still loveable,

Still gorgeous in somebody's, in my eyes,

Whereas I,

Am not gorgeous in anyone's.

Small

Their stares are like knifes as they watch my every move,

Going out is a challenge,

Facing people seems terrifying,

I want to let the fear consume me,

So scared of their stares,

So petrified of being judged,

Ten feet tall they rise up above,

Laughing as I fall to the ground,

So small and so afraid,

I am stuck on the ground,

Still despite being weak I continue to get back up,

They have a menacing laugh,

Evil eyes as they glare down at me,

And I know that I have no choice but to fight,

I may be weak,

I may be tired,

But still I know,

That I will win no matter what

To Him

To him she is gorgeous.

She is the sun in his world; his light.

To him she is the only person that keeps him alive.

She is a drug that he cannot help but be addicted to.

To her she is nothing in a world full of fascinating people.

To her he deserves better.

To him she is like the stars, shining bright in the dark, empty sky.

To her she is flawed and worthless.

She is holding him back; she is the clouds that get in the way.

She is a disease that only causes harm and anger.

She is something that needs to disappear.

To him she is a fallen angel.

To him he wants to be the knight that saves her from herself.

He wants to protect her from all the pain in the world.

But to her she is beyond saving.

She has already seen and experienced too much.

To him all he has to do is make her believe,

Once she believes in herself; when she sees he is truly, madly in love with her, she will be happy,
Yet in her eyes she is still nothing.

His Hands Are Shaking

His hands are shaking, as he holds his first gun,

Shoot the target they insist,

As he closes his eyes and wishes that he could be good.

His hands are shaking as he aims,

Ready to shoot the enemy; conditioned to see only through black and white,

"why hesitate?" The voice inside asks

His hands are shaking,

As he takes a life, somebody's brother, partner, son, or father, gone just like that,

How will this solve anything?

His hands are shaking,

Yet he stays quiet; he knows to listen to his orders.

His hands are shaking,

As he is at war with oneself

What gives him the right to take another's life?

What is there for him to live for after all? How can he fight when he is stuck at the bottom?

Bullets and wars are all he knows; where would he find love or salvation in a world full of hate?

His hands are shaking,

As he takes his final breathe,

Yet somewhere,

Someone's hands are shaking, as they find out the friend, brother, father, or partner has given up on hope for a better world.

Storm

The sun shines obnoxiously bright,

A cacophony of laughter and screams of happiness are heard,

Yet the clouds can be seen in the horizon,

Creeping nearer,

We know they are coming.

There is something missing,

Somewhere deep inside,

We are filled with melancholy,

The sun still shines brightly,

Yet the raindrops fall from the sky that slowly becomes dark as the clouds take over,

Sparkling like beautiful diamonds they fall,

Spreading sadness and heartbreak wherever they land,

Slowly we start to feel more and more empty,

Something makes the laughter sound less innocent and more sinister,

The sun becomes hidden behind clouds of despair,

And all that we are left with is darkness,

All of us wondering if it will ever be overcome by the light.

Suffocating

I'm falling,

You're laughing,

Not realising just how far I am sinking,   I
cannot swim.
Yet you expect me to be able to,

Without any help,

I'm struggling to breathe,

I'm trying to swim back up,

Yet all that happens is that more water gets into my mouth,

I keep my eyes shut tight,

Gasping for air,

Refusing to let the tears fall,

Not wanting to face the terrifying dark world around me,

I keep trying to swim,

But it's useless.

Slowly bit by bit I'm drowning,

Suffocating until I'm almost at the bottom.

Yet you still have not even realised just how far I have fallen

Flames

It was dark,

Then suddenly someone lit a flame,

It was so bright that suddenly everything seemed so much lighter,

No longer scared; I smiled,

Hope grew in my heart,

And the world seemed so much brighter,

Everything was perfect, just for a while,

I let myself become enthralled,

I was so intrigued; unable to turn away,

I could only move closer to the flame that seemed to make all of my darkness disappear,

Too naïve to see the warning signs,

Too young to see bad in anyone,

I got too close to the flame and got burned,

But still I stayed; not moving away,

And when eventually the flame died a part of me died with it,

All I was left with was emptiness and loneliness,

No one else cared for they couldn't understand why I had been so enthralled by the flame,

Why I hadn't left when the truth was right in front of me,

And so I cried, alone in the darkness,

Loneliness and insecurities were all I knew,

Until finally, slowly I started to become myself again,

A flame formed in my eyes,

And I no longer needed someone else to guide me,

As I found my own way out of the darkness.

Cracks

Staring into her reflection she screamed,

Cracks visible everywhere she turned,

Drops of blood visible on the floor,

She could not face them,

The demons laughed,

Knowing her weakness as always,

Taunting,

Laughing at her expense,

Fighting a battle inside her head for as long as she could remember,
And yet she was still stuck.   Still trapped,   Still lonely.
She told them that she was okay,

She was fine really,

And yet at night staring up at the ceiling,

She broke,

So lost, alone and pathetic,

She had so many people surrounding her,   Yet
it was never enough.
She needed everyone to love her

Even when all she saw when looking at herself were cracks

Flaws,

Imperfections,

She would never be enough,

Not to them

Not to herself.

Anxiety

I hear them whispering again,   What
can I do?
What can I do to make them let me go?

Chained inside the walls I built I am unable to escape,

They don't like me.

I don't either.

Yet I still need them to love me,

If they don't how can I do it?

How can I face them without their approval?

It's all in my head they say,

Yet could they ever understand?

The desperation,

The dread,

The fear of facing people that probably dislike me almost as much as I hate myself.

I feel sick,

I cannot do it,

I just want to hide from it all,

To run away to somewhere where I don't feel as though I have to try to please
everyone all the time.

Trapped

They pull me into the darkness,

My screams are ignored,

There is no way out,

I'm trapped,

All that I can hear are screams,

I can see other people hurting,

I need to help,

Yet I cannot escape,

I am unable to get free,

I need to get out from this hell,

I need to help them,

To save them from feeling the same hell that I do every day,   Yet,
how can I?
As they hold me against my will,

Breaking me down,

Until I am too scared to say or do anything except hide.

Bullets

I see bullets flying past me,

Every time that close my eyes,

Bodies falling to the ground,   How
will I ever move on?
Every morning I wake up from a nightmare,

A memory,

My heart breaks more and more every day,

I remember what once was,

I remember that day,

I remember running with only survival on my mind,

I was so selfish,

I should have done something,

The guilt is the worst kind of pain,

Living with the memories,

Seeing people whom I'd known my whole life slowly take their last breath,

I see it every time that I close my eyes,

I can still hear their screams,

Can still smell the blood,

I should have died that day,

Yet for some reason I survived,

But really a part of me did die,

As now I will never be the same again;

I wake up in the middle of the night crying,

I have a panic attack every time I go outside,

And all I can hear are bullets flying past me, All
I can see are the people that I lost.

Try to Break Me

You can scar me with your words,

Break me with your fists,

Make me feel useless and pathetic,

Tell me that I'm not worth it,

Leaving as many scars on me as you please,

You can try and make me fall,

You can laugh when on occasion I break down,

Hold it against me that you have the upper hand,

But let me remind you that you will not defeat me,

I might be broken, I might be damaged,

I may not be perfect, and I may not always be strong,

But I am determined to make it through this fight; I will win if it is the last thing I do,

You are not worth my tears or my time,

Go ahead and call me names,

Try to make me cry,

Try to break me through pain and laughter,

I don't care,

For I know that I will never give up, And
one day I will win.

The field

Sitting there I am surrounded by silence,

No one can bother me here,

The field is empty,

Isolated and peaceful,

It's comforting,

Just silence and grass surrounding me,

I can finally think clearly,

My demons gone for a while.

The grass is long enough to hide in,

The trees perfect to climb,

Looking around,

There are so many memories that this place holds,

Laughter, imagination, and happiness

As well as a few arguments, falls and tears,

The place where my childhood lives,

I may never be able to come back here again,

But still the memories will live on forever,

Though I may not be able to come back physically,

In my head it will always exist,

Reminding me in my darkest moments,   That
there is peace in this world.

Fly

Come out of the darkness,

There is a light to lead you,

Open your eyes and fly,

Be yourself for once,

Do not be afraid,

You can do this,

Stand back on your own feet,

Leave the demons and the past behind

No longer hiding,

Only happiness awaits,

Put away the weapons,

Break down the walls,

It's okay now,

You are not alone,

You are free,

Like a bird who has just learned to fly,

Take that first leap,

Soar high in the sky,

The worst is over now,

It is time to face the world

Fly

Falling apart

I watch as she falls apart,

Bit by bit,

There's nothing I can do

She's only human,

I watch helpless as she falls to pieces on the floor,

Her heart shattered,

Her arm bloody,

She is broken,

I watch as she seeks help,

Yet people look the other way,

She is alone,

She is scared, I try
to help,

But there isn't much I can really do,

I watch as they judge her,

Their words scarring her forever,

As she crumbles,

I can do nothing but watch and try desperately to help, Whilst
the world watches on without a care.

Depression

Mascara streams down her face,

As she stares back into the mirror,

Hopeless and alone,

Slowly dying in the prison, she built around herself,

Insecurities nagging in her ears,

She tries to rationalise,

But in her head, it's useless,

Everything's a mess,

Panic and depression consume her,

Terrified of facing the world,

No energy to do so,

She cries alone in her room,

Feeling sick and hopeless,

She wants love,

She wants comfort,

She wants help,

Yet it's easier said than done,

Facing the world seems impossible,

Help seems further away than ever,

And all she wants to do is let the darkness consume her and give in to her everpersistent thoughts.

Bullying

Call him a freak,

Call her a slut,

Call them emo's, goths or nerds,

Say that they are dumb,

Say that you are better,

Laugh and watch as they fall,

Hit them until they are down,

Watch and laugh as they fall,   What

do you get from it?

Watching them suffer,

Does it make you feel powerful?

Does it make you feel in control?

Do you feel cool laughing and watching whilst they crumble?

Whilst they fall deeper into darkness?

You watch and laugh with a sadistic smile and evil narrowed eyes,

You want to feel strong; you want to feel better,   Are

you intimidated?

Will you feel regret, sorrow, or remorse when you see the terrible impact you have made?

I think that you are just a coward,

Hurting those around you just to fill the void,

Just to make it so that you are not the only one hurting,   But

really all it does is make you become more and more broken,

It isn't too late to change; just stand up and make a difference.

Just try to fix your mistakes and make a choice to be better.

Lost

I need help; melancholy is consuming me,

Thoughts of what would happen if I died overtake my mind,

They say that I can talk to them; so, I try,

I try to explain the numbness to them,

The fear I have of living in this world,

Yet they still don't seem to listen,

I'm more afraid of living then dying,

Yet I'm clearly being overdramatic,

How could anyone feel that way at eleven?

Clearly, I just want attention,

No one quite understands,

Everyone turns a blind eye,

I'm fed up and drained,

I feel numb, lost and broken,

And I'm not really sure why,

They don't understand how hard I'm trying just to keep my head above water,

Things were going so well,

And now I'm in yet another downward spiral,

I stay awake every night,

I try to read to distract myself from the terrible thoughts, but I eventually get bored,

And at three a.m. I lay in bed staring at the ceiling; no tears fall from my eyes and yet I feel like crying,

The world seems to be falling apart before my very eyes,
I think of all the people suffering,
And I think of how selfish I am for been upset and lost when I don't even know the reason.

Forget

Another shot

Another drink,

One more and I'll be okay.

I'll forget,

No one will matter anymore,

I forget my worries,

I forget my past,

And all of a sudden, I'm okay,

Just for a little while,

I forget about all my sadness,

All of my anxiety and panic are gone,

I'm happy,

With no cares or responsibilities,

No one to impress; there's just myself,

I can be who I am,

I can be the person I was meant to be before the darkness took me away

I can dance, smile and just be confident without wanting to run and hide,   I can finally be free

Just Put on a Smile

They say that it will be okay in the end,

That I am the one that needs to stay strong,

Be rational,

Be kind and be loyal,

Even when everyone else leaves,

When everyone else fights and screams,

I must just put on a smile,

Yet all I want to do is cry,

No matter how hard I try I cannot be enough,

I try and I try but to no avail,

And all I want to do is run away from it all,

I do not know how I can help,

I don't have enough money,

I am not clever enough to think of new ideas,

I am not brave or selfless enough,

Other people terrify me,

Their opinions, their thoughts, and their actions,

All makes me want to hide,

I feel crazy sometimes,

When I lose control and cry,

And I feel useless most of the time, As

I watch the world go on in pain,

Yet there doesn't seem to be anything that I can do,

To help them even just a little bit.

There Once Was a Girl

There once was a girl who was scared,

She was afraid that she would never find a happy ending,

For she had experienced so much pain that she no longer believed in love,

There once was a girl who learned to smile through the pain,

She had been through the good,

She had been through the bad,   And

as life knocked her down,

Again and again,

The girl learned to get up,

The girl learned to love herself,

She learned to love the world,

And with a determination of steel,

The girl fought to be happy,

She fought her demons with every bit of strength she had,   And
slowly she learned to rise above the darkness

Nothing

Pulled back to the dark once again she screams,

It consumes her as she goes back in time

All of a sudden, she is a lost little girl once again hiding away from the world,

Stuck in the dark

All alone with nowhere to turn the thoughts invade her mind:

She is useless, a waste of space,

She cannot escape

Her own mind is once again her enemy for reasons she cannot seem to fathom,

She cries in bed alone as she watches the world go by,

No one coming to save her and no idea of how to save herself,

She gets the knife and does the only thing she knows how to make herself feel,

Only to be left with irreversible damage,

Blood drips from her arm yet she still feels numb,

It made things worse as it always did,

Relapsing

For the first time in years only to feel number than ever,

She puts on some music to drown out the thoughts,

Yet it doesn't help

Stuck with her own thoughts she doesn't know how to escape from herself, And so, she falls,
The numbness consumes her and once again she is nothing.

Those Days

Do you remember the days when we were so close?

Remember when we thought that we were invincible?

Laughing and drinking till we forgot our names we were happy,

We thought that we would never grow apart,

Life was never perfect but all that we needed was each other,

But then one day everything fell apart,

The laughter faded to silence and the happiness to sadness,

I knew that it was coming yet I was still in shock,

We were invincible once,

We could be like that again,

Tell me do you not remember?

We could get through anything as long as we had each other,

But then came that day,

You packed your bags and left me with the promise that I would be okay,

And for some reason I believed you,

When really, I should have fought for you to stay,

The memory will always haunt me,

And right now, I just really need you,

Because together we were invincible

Nobody

I tried to help you,

But instead I'm the one that got burnt,

You never needed me,

Not really,

I wanted to help people,

To make them happy,

To make you happy,

But really, I'm useless,

Because no matter how hard I try I will never mean anything to any of you,

I'm just another face amongst the people you see in the crowd,

Someone you pass on the street,

Sit next to on the bus,

I wanted to be somebody,

I wanted to matter,

I tried to help people I work with,

People I see every day,

I tried to make friends,

But I will never be anyone,

Not in your eyes,

I'll always just be that girl that tries too hard,   That
no one really wants.

Alone

I hate being alone,

So I go out and pretend to be someone else,

I try to fit in,

To do anything to make people love me,

And yet nothing ever works,

Whether I'm myself or someone else entirely,

I'm no one,

I go home alone,

An empty house awaiting me,

I wake up with nothing on my phone,

The silence is more deafening then anything you could possibly imagine,

I try to block it out,

I try to block out the sounds of other people laughing,

Talking,

Making friends,

Because I will always be the one left behind,

The one that no one really loves nor wants,

So I give up,

And I give in to the silence,

Music my only company,
All I want is love,
Maybe I just don't deserve it after all.

Save Me

I want someone to save me,

To help,

For someone just to realize how lost I am,

I need someone to wake me up from this nightmare,

To realise how fake my smile is,

How hard depression has hit me at just eleven years old,

But no one ever looks past the facade,

I don't know how to save myself,

I don't know how to get help,

Because I really don't know why I'm so broken,

I don't know how to put it into words,

A part of me just wishes that someone could see right through my smile,

Look at me and see the truth,

And that they would save me,

But after all this time no one's done that,

And all I know now is how to lock people out,

How to put up walls to hide how I really feel,

I still want someone to save me,

A part of me still wants to trust,

To believe the best,

But after been knocked down so many times,

I don't know how to get back up anymore.

Afraid

Listen to music

Read a book,

Watch something,

Just block them out, they say,

Like it's so easy,

My greatest enemy is myself,

I try to get rid of my thoughts,

Yet nothing helps,

Sitting in the darkness I cry,

Wondering if and when it will ever get better,

Desperate and afraid,

I don't want to be like this forever,

Broken and damaged,

Tears escape my eyes,

I listen to that voice inside my head,

Let my depression and anxiety control me,

On yet another path of self-destruction,

But if no one else cares then why should I?

Self-Destruct

Staring back at herself,

She breaks,

Useless and fed up with feeling like nothing,

She hits self-destruct yet again,

The red button in her head so tempting,

So alluring,

She gives up on fighting,

She puts all her energy into pretending,

So, at night she had no energy left to block them out,

No energy to face them,

And so, she breaks more and more,

Not eating throughout the day,

No choice but to power through,

Hating every part of herself,

Despite how beautiful she really was,

She could not see it,

Could only see the fat,

Could only see the scars,

She could only see the hopelessness in her eyes,   And all she felt was defeat.

Toxic

Our love was crazy,

Toxic,

Poisonous,

You made me feel as though I were drowning most of the time,

But sometimes you were my light too,

Guiding me back through the darkest of times,

You were my hero when you wanted to be,

My happiness,

My peace,

My clarity,

I stopped listening to my head,

Only focusing on the rare moments in which you made me happy,

Denial consumed me,

Because you were my world,

Helping me pick up the pieces,

Only to be the one to throw them back on to the floor,

I couldn't understand,

Why you hurt me again and again,

Why you had to lie to me when I would have given you everything,

But I couldn't see,

How toxic you were to me,

How each time you broke me,

You took a part of me with you.

Remembrance Day

They died for us,

Fighting a seemingly never-ending war,

Loyal soldiers fighting a battle just so that we could have our freedom,

Taking bullets,

Crying as they took their last breath,

Hopelessness filling them each night,

Wondering if they would ever return home,

Deemed weak if they showed signs of not wanting to fight,

They fought each day for the world in which we now live in,

Wondering if they were making the right decision,

As they prepared for battle,

Wondering if those on the other side,

Were just as conflicted, just as confused and lost,

Looking at pictures and letters from loved ones,

They told themselves to have hope,

One day it will be over,

One day someone will win,

But really it never seemed to end,

And those lucky enough to return home were forever scarred and lost,

Remembering their friends and lovers they fought on for years,

Until finally it came to an end,

And still the world cried,

For innocent people died on the battlefield, surrounded by Poppy's.

<h1 style="text-align:center">How to Say Goodbye</h1>

I still don't know how to say goodbye,

Soon it will have been a year,

A year since you left me,

A year since cancer took you away,

You were my hero,

My best friend,

And whilst everyone seems to be moving on,

I find myself stuck in the past,

Memories haunt me,

I don't ever want to ever forget you,

I just want the pain to go away,

You wouldn't have wanted this for me,   But

what do I do with you gone?

How do I keep going?

Without you to guide me I'm lost,

You kept me going for years,

You were there when I had nowhere else to turn,

And now I find myself looking for you all the time,

Only to remember that you are gone,

Still in my heart as you always will be,

But gone from this word,

And I don't know how to cope with that.

Unheard

Unwanted, unheard, she sits on her own,

Forever silenced she cries in the dark,

Unloved and misheard she tries to speak,

Only to be cut down by those surrounding her,

Surrounded by them, she attempts to fight,

Still showing no mercy they push her to the ground,

Get up, she says as she holds her head high,

Don't let them win,

For they are the monsters in this world,

Surrounded again she attempts to stand up,

Be tall and be proud,

However, they tower over,

Push her to the ground again and again,

Up she rises straight after she falls,

Wiping her tears,

Walking through fire,

Unbeaten, undefeated,   They
will not win.
Again, and again she gets back up,   Again,

and again she rises above,

Again, and again the cycle goes,

Only to finally stop once they see,   Just
how unheard they are to her.

Rise

Miss-understood she weeps as she locks the door,

Forever alone in a world full of hate,

She breathes and tells herself soon, she will be fine,

The moment will pass and once again she will be strong,

She rises up again as she goes back,

Back into the hell that made her lose control,

Seemingly calm she smiles through hell,

Rising up each time that the demons call,

Ignoring them she stays calm,

Internally fighting,

The battle in her head,

She will win,

She continues to rise as she fights back,

Strong and determined,

She will win,

Rising again she promises herself,

She will breathe when she feels lost and alone,   The

demons will be defeated once and for all,

She will continue to rise as the demons fall,

At last she wins as she fights to the end,

Rising up she is happy, after winning the fight,
The demons that linger, ignored, and pushed back,
For she will rise again each time they make her fall.

Butterfly

Trapped in a cage,

Unable to fly,

A butterfly cries as it tries to escape,

Locked away safely,

Something to look at,

Stuck all alone,

It is afraid and sad,

People stare at its beauty,

Unable to comprehend,

That the beautiful butterfly is trapped and alone,

Stuck in a cage, the key long gone,

The butterfly cries as it tries to escape,

There for amusement,

For beauty and decoration,

The butterfly is unable to fly,

Trapped in its cage,

Giving up it sits,

Defeated and sad,

Only for someone to look and say no,

Finally, someone comes and lets it free,

And the butterfly flies as the butterfly is free,

Far more beautiful it is in the wild,

Finally, free, finally happy, the butterfly flies out in the wild.

On the Streets

On the streets stuck,

They stare up ahead,

Passing them by without a care in the world,

No conversation,

No food and no hope,

Giving up he/ she cries,

On the streets all alone as people pass by,

Making sure they don't look,   For
how could they face them?
The ones who are lost and alone,

Shunned by society,

Judged on their status,

No home and no food,

No money, no job,

They are stuck all alone,

Some turn to addiction,

Some turn to depression,

Some turn to death as the hunger becomes too much,

Not their fault, but society's for throwing them out,

After trying their best, they are thrown to the streets,

Alone and cold they stare on ahead,

As the loneliness grows, people walk on; not wanting, not willing to help those on the ground.

Come Together

Fear consumes her as she looks out,

The world is on fire, the people crying,

All is a nightmare in reality,

People begging on the streets with no shelter to sleep,

She wants to do something as she watches on in horror,

People starving,

People crying as the world crumbles,

Miss-communication and miss-understandings,

The world is messy and is falling apart,

She watches as the children cry and as people get lost,

Financial, physical, or psychological – something is wrong,

Everyone is lost as it continues,

Unsure how to fix themselves, unsure how to fix each other,

She does what she can, and so do they,

Stuck at the bottom and turned against each other,

No one can do much,

They watch on in terror as children starve,

As mothers cry and fathers cry, there seems to be no hope,

If they come together, maybe they will make a difference,

If they come together for once they will help each other,

Angry and hurt, everyone is all alone,

Traumatic pasts, traumatic lives; they need help,

Alone and screaming they are pushed to the ground,

Be the one to help each other rise and stand back up after someone is knocked to
the ground.